W9-DJF-829

SMILE!
by
Bil Keane

A FAWCETT GOLD MEDAL BOOK

Fawcett Publications, Inc., Greenwich, Connecticut

A School Book Fairs, Inc. Edition

"HOME TILL SEPTEMBER!"

"Mommy, could you drive me over to the school yard to play?"

"But I told all the guys that when school was out you'd let me stay up to watch Johnny Carson."

"Because I don't wanna spend the first day of my summer vacation in BED!"

"Calm down! CALM DOWN! We don't leave on vacation till SATURDAY!"

"When are we leaving, Daddy? I'VE been ready since breakfast."

"Mommy, can Kathy go on vacation with us? She
wouldn't take up much room."

"29,999.9 — Now watch, everybody — there it
goes! 30,000.0! Hold it there, Daddy! Look at all the
ZEROES!"

"Why are you going so slow, Daddy? We'll NEVER get there."

"There's ANOTHER one and ANOTHER! Aw, Daddy,
can't you steer around those poor bugs?"

"Aw! Do we hafta stop and get out again, Daddy?"

"Stop botherin' Daddy, Jeffy! Move over. Don't touch Daddy's arm, Jeffy! You're bein' a nuisance, right, Daddy?"

"PJ can't go in there! He's not a GIRL!"

"Ahhh! Feels good to sit down!"

"Mommy, will you tell Jeffy to stop bumping me while I'm crayoning?"

"Hold it! There's no TV in this place."

"Time for vacation to begin, Daddy."

"Let's just forget about having a fire in the fireplace."

"Mommy, will you get everybody out of my way? I want to jump rope."

"Why haven't you caught any fish, Daddy?"

"Daddy, you have some dirt right here."

"That's a MOUSTACHE! I've been waiting for somebody to notice."

"What's so funny? A lot of guys grow moustaches
while they're on vacation."

"... Four ... five ... WOW! Daddy made that
stone skip SIX times! How many can YOU
do, Mommy?"

"Aren't we going to the BEACH this year?"

"Back from the hike already?"

"THERE they are, Daddy! There are those fishies we
were tryin' to catch!"

"This is MY side of the road. You look on your side."

"Why CAN'T we, Mommy?"

"If I pretend I'm asleep, too, do I get carried in?"

"Why do you keep saying I'm ready for a vacation, Mommy? We just GOT BACK from one."

"...And here's where I fell off a log and this is from swimmin' into a rock and here's some ivy poison and..."

"Could I kiss you on the cheek, Daddy? That
'stache HURTS."

"IT makes you
look old."

"Mommy! He shaved
it off!"

"Mommy, will you fill up this 'nana skin again?"

"All right—avocado. But, when I was a little girl it was just plain green."

"Mommy! Is my watch waterproof? Jeffy SNEEZED on it!"

"Daddy forgot to kiss Teddy goodby."

"Ask your mother if we can climb on your roof."

"Okay, But I hope she says no."

"Daddy, how old were you when Mommy let you cut up your own meat?"

"Why don't we just put a sign on the gate, 'No strange doggies allowed.'"

"If you really like the picture I drew, Grandma, how come you hung it inside your closet door?"

"Wanna try it, Daddy? It's fun!"

"Practice faster, Billy. We can't turn on TV till
you're finished."

"This is the house that Jack built. This is the malt that
lay in the house that Jack built. This is the rat   that
ate the malt that lay in the house that Jack built. THIS
is the cat that killed the rat that ..."

"How 'bout THIS one, Mommy?"

"Why don't you retire from work now, Daddy, before you're too old to play with us?"

"I like printing better than writing 'cause you can rest between letters."

"Mommy! The moon just landed! Can we go over to the airport to see it?"

"Mommy, do I know how to read?"

"If we're eating with KNIVES and FORKS, why do I
have to wash my HANDS?"

"If you're late for work do you have to report to the boss's office?"

"When I wear this muscle shirt Grandma sent me, do I need pants on or not?"

"You can come in now. I've finished my piano practice."

"Mommy, what would be a good name for a toad?"

"You mean you don't even know 'My Country Tis of Thee' when you hear it, Jeffy?"

"Ask Mommy to come and be the chipmunk. Your voice isn't squeaky enough."

"Grandma, why don't you ever give Mommy and Daddy any dimes?"

"Mommy wants us to make up our minds BEFORE **!**
open up the door!"

"Mommy, how do you spell P.S.?"

"Do I hafta get the child's plate? I'm SEVEN!"

"Mommy, are Barfy and Sam the same religion as we are?"

"It's strange how much heavier he is at night than in the morning."

"Are you sure you looked real good? Sometimes
Mommy HIDES the cookies."

"In the future you're to stay away — here's another one — from the sandbox when you're wearing beads."

"Leave the front and back the way it is and nothing off the top and sides, please."

"Mommy! I don't care for all of this hamburger!"

"I know where spring, summer, fall and winter are, but I can't figure out where AUTUMN fits in."

"Does it hurt your head when you turn somersaults?"

" 'Cause I didn't think of toasting it until AFTER I put the peanut butter on it."

"Mommy's throwin' away your old fishin' rod! Do you
want us to get it back for you?"

"Bless Mommy and Daddy and all those other people
in last night's prayer."

"Daddy bought some STRAWS! Can we have a soda
to test them out?"

"We were ALMOST good. Do we still get a surprise?"

"Daddy, will you make Billy stop coughing? He's keepin' me awake."

"How could I have chicken pox? I wasn't even NEAR a chicken!"

"I wish they never invented chicken pox."

"Mommy! Come quick! Billy's SCRATCHIN' his chick-
en pops!"

"Billy's LUCKY! He gets his meals on a tray, Daddy brings him presents, he watches TV all day . . ."

". . . And nobody can go near Billy 'cept Mommy 'cause she's a MUNE."

"Don't touch! That's Billy's tray and it's full of
chicken pops!"

"I'm feelin' better. Mommy took my temperature and it's down to zero."

"I'm tellin'! You're going out of bounds with the red!"

"Wow! I think I'm rich 'cause I can't lift my bank."

"They DID!"
"DIDN'T"
"DID!"
"DIDN'T!"

"Mommy, when the dish ran away with the spoon, did they get married or not?"

"Mommy! I found the peanut brittle!"

"Mommy! The phone wants you!"

"Jeffy called this peach a plum! Boy! He sure
doesn't know his vegetables!"

"Mommy! Daddy's playing in his office clothes!"

"I like LAND food better — hamburgers, hot dogs..."

"Deep end! I get in the deep end!"

"My eyes are getting tired watching for Daddy to come home."

"What I like best about church is when the organ
makes the whole place shake!"

"Mommy, can you be-tend you're a little girl and play house with me?"

"What does K-K-A-A-A spell, Daddy?"

"Grandma says there are a lot of cal'ries in ice cream, but I can't find a ONE."

"Mommy, how long till you give me back my roller skates?"

"Shall I throw this bike away? The bell's broken."

"Whisper on THIS side — I'm left-eared."

"This is what they mean by 'puttin' something away for a rainy day,' right, Mommy?"

"How many more fingers do I hafta be till I'm as old as Billy?"

"My monkey did it."

"The party's not over yet — I just came home to get
my siren and handcuffs."

"The big hand's on one and the little hand is on nine and the red hand is on two, three, four, five . . ."

"Oh, boy! Can I sit next to the groceries?"

"Hi, Daddy! Mommy's takin' a shower, but you can
hug and kiss me instead till she gets through."

"You better do what Mommy tells you — if you know what side your bread is peanut-buttered on."

"Both our dresses are the same 'cept Mommy's has more curves and things."

"We'll help you decide what to fix for lunch — How
'bout cake and ice cream?"
"How 'bout root beer and cookies?"
"How 'bout. . ."

"Mommy! My lob went over the net!"

"The 'lectricity is off because of the storm and we get
to eat all the ice cream in the freezer!"

"Know why I like breakfast best? We don't have to eat any vegetables."

Mommy, a caterpurtle wants to know if he can come
into our house. Can he?"

"Come quick, Mommy. The picture's wrinkled!"

"Just eat it, Jeffy—your tummy won't know the difference."

"Robert used a bad word! And it wasn't just a
children's bad word, it was a GROWN-UP's bad
word!"

"Oh boy! My favorite! Pasghetti and meat bulbs!"

"Skip the next part, Daddy, and start where the bunny rabbit goes into the barn."

"Look what the dumb ol' driveway did to my pants."

"Mommy, Dolly's hickin' ups."

"Wait till I grow up! I'll ride all the way down the street to the McCormicks'—maybe even to the Pooles'—maybe even across Woodland Road!"

"I hope I don't marry somebody with a long name
'cause I'll NEVER learn to spell it."

"Hey! That's the face Mommy drew with icing on our cookies!"

"Jack and Jill were over the hill . . ."

"Billy's washing, I'm drying and Jeffy's pickin' up the pieces."

"Billy's not here, so can I have HIS cookie?"

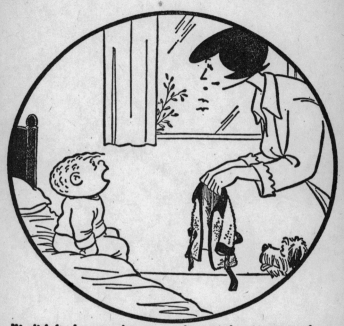

"I didn't dream about you last night, Mommy, but
don't worry — I'll dream about you tomorrow."